Day Trading

Trade the Stock Market Like a Pro

By

John Gibson

Copyright 2018 by John Gibson - All rights reserved.

The following book is reproduced below with the goal of providing information that is as accurate and reliable as possible. Regardless, purchasing this book can be seen as consent to the fact that both the publisher and the author of this book are in no way experts on the topics discussed within and that any recommendations or suggestions that are made herein are for entertainment purposes only. Professionals should be consulted as needed prior to undertaking any of the action endorsed herein.

This declaration is deemed fair and valid by both the American Bar Association and the Committee of Publishers Association and is legally binding throughout the United States.

Furthermore, the transmission, duplication or reproduction of any of the following work including specific information will be considered an illegal act irrespective of if it is done electronically or in print. This extends to creating a secondary or tertiary copy of the work or a recorded copy and is only allowed with express written consent from the Publisher. All additional right reserved.

The information in the following pages is broadly considered to be a truthful and accurate account of facts and as such any inattention, use or misuse of the information in question by the reader will render any resulting actions solely under their purview. There are no scenarios in which the publisher or the original author of this work can be in any fashion deemed liable for any hardship or damages that may befall them after undertaking information described herein.

Additionally, the information in the following pages is intended only for informational purposes and should thus be thought of as universal. As befitting its nature, it is presented without assurance regarding its prolonged validity or interim quality. Trademarks that are mentioned are done without written consent and can in no way be considered an endorsement from the trademark holder.

Table of Contents

Chapter 1: The Basics- Trends and Ranges _____ 6

Chapter 2: Turning Points _____ 13

Chapter 3: Stock Market Mechanics _____ 17

Chapter 4: The MACD- Improved _____ 23

Chapter 5: 20 EMA S/R _____ 29

Chapter 6: Momentum Patterns _____ 33

Chapter 7: Volume Analysis _____ 45

Chapter 8: Accumulation and Distribution _____ 56

Chapter 9: Risk Management _____ 59

Chapter 11: How to Make Millions _____ 78

Introduction

Hello there. Thank you for buying this book. Chances are you have some knowledge of the financial markets and have some experience trading them whether as a beginner, an expert or as is most common, the frustrated semi professional. The odds are also good that the biggest reason you decided to start trading in the first place is because of the massive financial rewards it offers. You may be passionate about the markets and the way they work but, to be honest, passion doesn't quite match the feeling of knowing you can make a living in the markets and that you can rely upon yourself to create a richer life using your skills in trading.

Well, I'm here to hammer a few home truths into you. Yes, trading offers massive financial rewards. Rewards which only a few can ever hope to achieve. Getting there though is a function of passion, hard work and time. If you're expecting millions per month after reading a book like this, well, you're probably better off "investing" in the hot business idea du jour. Let me make this clear: To obtain the rewards you need to master a variety of skills. Technical skills, Risk management skills and most importantly mindset.

The good news is this: Trading successfully is a process. It involves executing a number of steps perfectly and managing your expectations regarding outcomes you have no control over. It involves understanding the risks you undertake every time you sit to trade and mitigating them as best as you can. It involves training yourself to be aware of what is inside your head and how that affects you. This book, the first of a series, is an attempt to demystify these 3 skills of successful trading across all markets and instruments. In this book, we will focus on the stock market and how to successfully day trade it.

We will first look at some basic concepts which you need to understand before we dive into the mechanics and peculiarities of the stock markets and then look at technical methods of developing an edge in the markets. After that, we will look at risk management techniques and round it all off with a brief look at mindset management. The topic of mindset is beyond the scope of this book since, that alone is something which will fill out entire volumes.

Do whatever you need to do to understand the material in here. Study it, print it out, buy a print version and re-read it multiple times. This is a very dense book and some topics will take time to understand, especially the basics. With that being said: I wish you the best of luck in your journey to trade successfully. Always remember: You're a lot closer than you believe. Always.

Chapter 1: The Basics- Trends and Ranges

"The trend is your friend", "Always trade with the trend", "Always take the path of least resistance". These are some home truths always spewed by the trading "authorities" everywhere. While these statements have their origin in fact, most of these authorities conveniently forget to mention the most basic of questions: What is a trend and how do I identify the direction?

You've probably read some variation of this piece of advice in answer to that question: "Well just look left to right in the chart! Is it going up? Then you're in an uptrend! Down? You're in a downtrend! Simple!". If there was a prize awarded for the most useless pieces of advice ever given, this one would be right up there with "Yes, its a great idea to meddle with Middle Eastern politics."

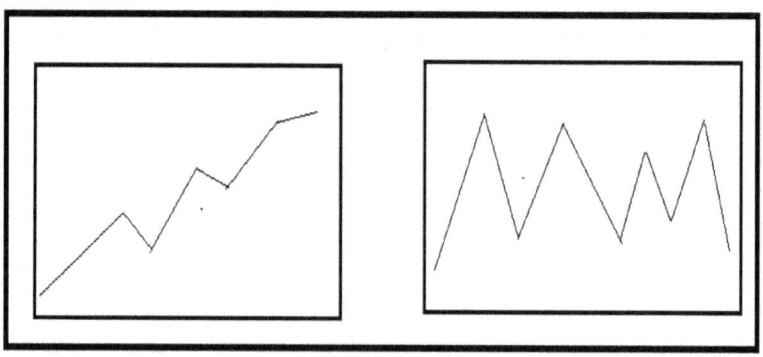

Figure 1: Look, a trend on the left and a range on the right! How simple is this? If only real world charts were this easy

Now don't misunderstand me. These statements have some truth to them but they completely neglect to mention something that is critical to your success in the markets: *The strength of the trend.*

What do I mean by trend strength? Simply put, its the degree to which order flow is tilted in favor of a given direction. You will always find trends which have some degree of imbalance between the bulls and bears. Order flow which is completely tilted towards the bulls results in a trend which is extremely bullish. Similarly, order flow which is completely tilted towards the bears will result in a trend which is extremely bearish. The majority of the time, order flow is distributed in some proportion between bulls and bears. Understanding the proportion is key to successful trading.

It follows from the above paragraph that order flow which is equally divided results in a range. In other words, a range is the result completely balanced order flow. This is where the market goes sideways and there isn't any apparent direction. For a market to have direction, there needs to be an imbalance in the order flow.

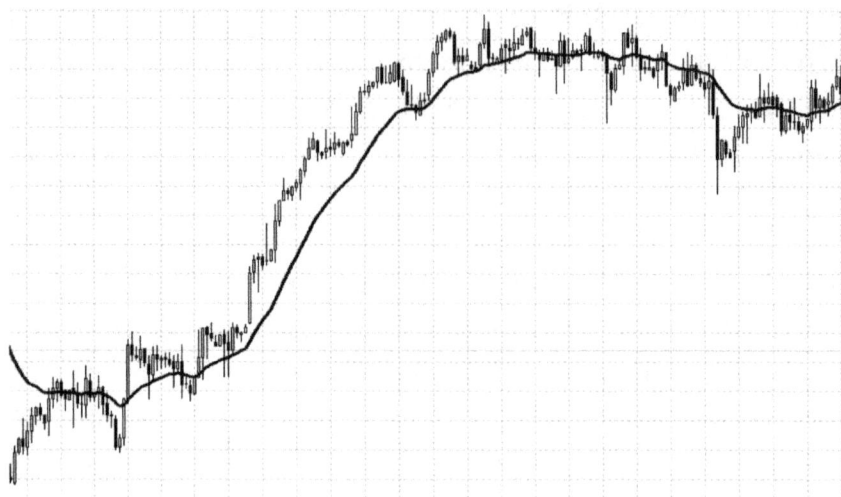

Figure 2: A great example of trend strength changing. Note the size of the bearish bars compared to the bullish ones on the left of the chart and notice how the bullish bars steadily increase compared to the bearish ones in both size and number. Observe the number of full bodies bullish bars compared to the bearish ones. In the middle of the picture, there's a complete lack of bearish bars and bullish trend strength is very high. As we move to the right, the bears re enter and the picture gets flipped as compared to the left. It is now the bears who are exerting greater pressure and the order flow becomes more balanced and tilted towards the bears despite price continuing to be in an uptrend. The trend strength here is very low for obvious reasons.

Now that we've defined what is meant by the strength of a trend, what are some ways we can assess it? Well, since trends are a result of order flow imbalances, it follows that the percentage of bearish orders versus bullish orders will give us the degree to which the market is imbalanced. Thankfully, due to the advent of charts we can do this visually. The following list is a brief method of identifying trend strength:

1) Is price going up or down when seen left to right?

2) What is the proportion of bull candles to bear candles? (or bars if you're so inclined)

3) How frequent are the bullish and bearish candles?

4) What is size of the bullish versus the bearish candles?

5) How much do the bear candles push back into the bull candles and vice versa?

Sometimes, the degree of pushback into the trend will be huge. Such an occurrence gives us an indication that the trend might be about to flip over to the other side. If you've ever wondered which side of the market to trade, you will appreciate the significance of that statement. Now, not all charts will be simple or clear to you especially if you're starting out. This is where chart time and experience comes in. Clarity in this regards is simply a function of the number of hours you spend analyzing a chart. The more you practice this skill, the easier it becomes. In case the chart on a particular timeframe is unclear, my advice is to simply go up one timeframe. So for example if the 5 minute chart seems muddled, switch to a 15 minute chart and so on. Another indicator which often helps with this is the 20 bar exponential moving average.

The 20 EMA is useful not because 20 is a magic number. It is useful because a large majority of traders use it. Please note though that the 20 EMA is a tool and not a crutch. You should avoid using it as a sole indicator except in a very special case as explained later. If the picture is muddled, then see if price is above or below the 20 EMA. This will clear it up a bit. So to re-iterate, the visual way where we look at the frequency and size and pushback of the bars is the best way. You can however take the help of the higher timeframe and 20 EMA sometimes.

Markets will often go sideways, that is, the order flow will be completely balanced. Such situations are referred to as ranges and its tempting to think of them as directionless. Some traders will even use this to justify trading both sides of a range, that is, going long and short. This is a bad idea for a beginner to do, in my opinion, since it is almost certain that a beginner will apply this logic in a formulaic way. The reality is far more nuanced than this.

While the range itself indicates balanced order flow, one must keep in mind that the order flow is balanced for that particular timeframe. The higher timeframe, which will always trump the lower one, may be indicating something entirely different.

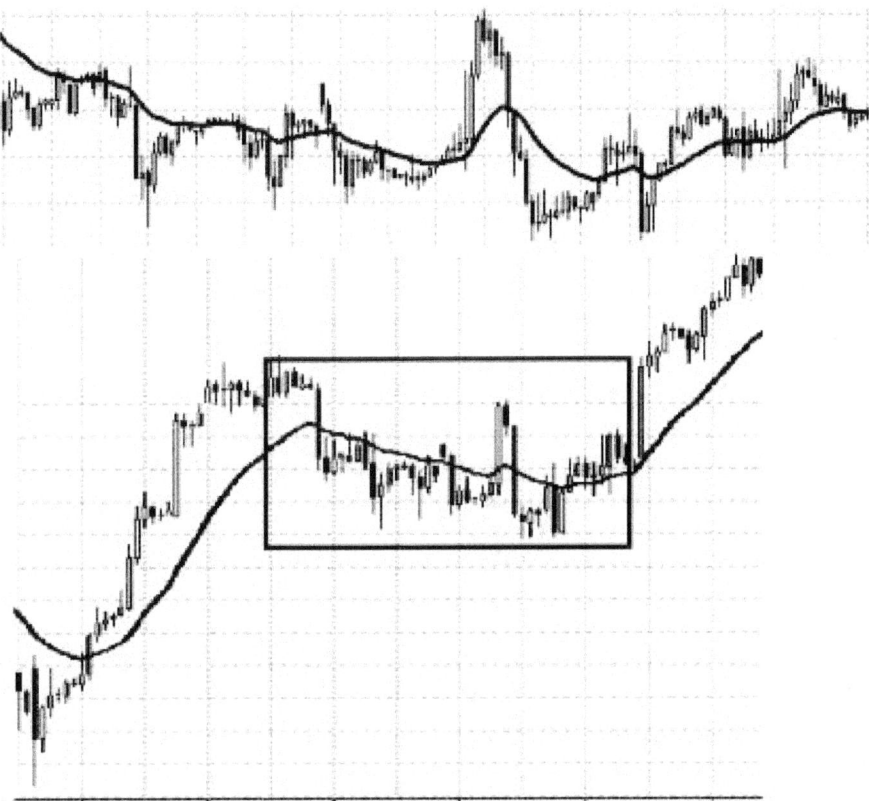

Figure 3: Timeframes matter. The picture on the top depicts a range on the 1 hour timeframe for the DAX. You'd think you can play both sides. However, looking the higher timeframe, the 4 hour chart at the bottom, its obvious the DAX is in an uptrend.
Taking a short is simply going against the odds or the line of least resistance or whatever you want to call it.

In such situations its important to recognize the following: The current timeframe may be indicating range but the higher timeframe indicates a strong uptrend. There is no contradiction here. The markets are a chaotic place and you will often see the higher timeframe completely contradict the lower one. This has major implications for our understanding of trading with trends.

Trend trading is more than just looking left to right and blindly determining the direction and placing a trade. We need to also take into account what the higher timeframe is indicating. If the 5 minute indicates a bull trend and the 15 minute indicates a bear trend, placing a buy order (long) on the 5 minute makes that order a countertrend order. Re read that again and let it sink in. Chances are you've never read it before.

There are times though, as mentioned previously, where the order flow seems to completely turn the other way and becomes imbalanced towards the opposite direction. Now the visual inspection method says we need to look left to right and look at the nature of the bars etc but sometimes it just seems obvious that the current trend is not very strong at all. In other words, how do know when the trend has ended and flipped the other way? This is what is addressed in the next chapter.

Chapter 2: Turning Points

The previous chapter was about identifying trends and how the underlying order flow indicates what direction the market is headed in. However, all things come to an end. Successful trading requires us to be able to identify in advance when a trend might be coming to an end so as to enable us to switch sides in the market. Not having this skill will leave us trading the wrong side of the market and no amount of hard work will ensure success in such a scenario.

Its important to remember before we proceed that the markets are chaotic and it doesn't make sense to expect a clean and clear signal. This "Holy Grail" approach to things is what dooms most beginners and causes them to chase that perfect indicator or pattern or setup. The reality is no such thing exists. Even when evaluating trends and the general pattern of the market, you must keep in mind, we aren't trying to unlock some secret code. We're merely trying to get a good idea of which way order flow is headed. If we cannot figure this out with clarity, it makes no sense to participate in the market at that given moment.

The strength of the trend, as explained in the previous chapter, gives us an idea of how many buyers and sellers are present at a given time. Now, when a trend starts to reverse , the number of counter trend players increase. This translates as more counter trend bars on the price chart and hence, a more balanced order flow i.e an equal number of bulls and bears.

Eventually, the counter players overwhelm the incumbent trend players and then the trend reverses.

This doesn't mean that every trend is followed by a range and that range is followed by a reversal. That is too simplistic a view for a chaotic environment. However, this holds largely true across all instruments and environments and markets. Remember though, while the order flow may have reversed on a lower timeframe, the higher timeframe may indicate the opposite. That is, you could see a bear trend start on the 5 minute chart but the 15 minute chart still shows a range. Trading such environments, where the lower and higher timeframes don't agree with one another, is something addressed in the next chapter.

So now, we can reasonably spot the possible end of a trend before it actually does using the trend strength approach. It is necessary though to draw a line in the sand and designate an area on the chart beyond which, we will know for certain that the trend has reversed. This is because while the order flow may indicate something, an unforseen event may cause the existing trend to continue. Or simply put, we might be incorrect in our reading of the market.

This line in the sand is essentially a turning point where we flip our bias on the market and start trading the other side in earnest. It is saying "If price goes below XX, I'm switching my bias to bearish from bullish and will go short below that level and remain long above it." So what do these turning points look like on a chart? The most common types are swing highs or lows, a prior range or a level which is present (as a range of swing point) on both the current and higher timeframe.

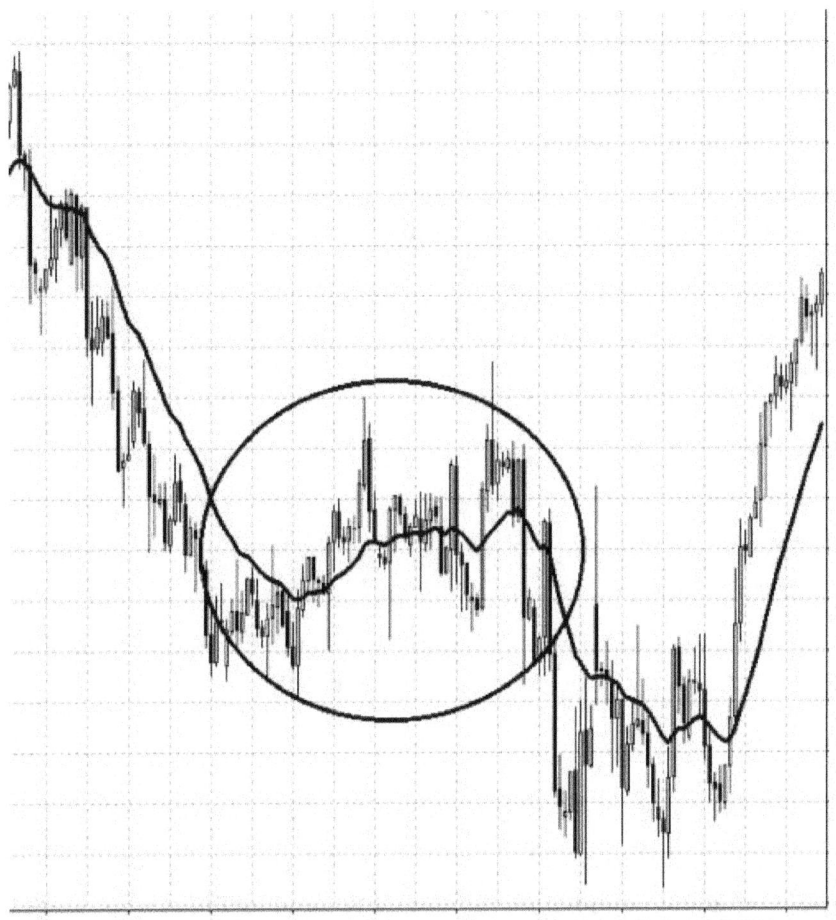

Figure 4: Compare the nature of the buying before versus after and inside the circle. The bullish bars are more frequent and larger in size indicating increasing buying interest. Price ultimately reverses and is in a full fledged bull trend once it clears the prior highs within the circle.

It is important to distinguish an ordinary swing level versus a key swing level to designate as a turning point. In Figure 4, we can see a range before price ultimately reverses but designating the top of this range as a turning point would be incorrect. This is because prior to this, we had a bigger range, denoted by the circle, where buyers showed up in big numbers and were rejected strongly by the sellers. It stands to reason that this level is a well defended one. Therefore, if the buyers can break through this level, the sellers will most likely wave a white flag. Hence, we designate the top of the prior range as the turning point.

Such a reading of the market takes time to build up to and a lot of practice. The rewards are huge though. More than any indicator, this is what will guide you towards the correct direction of trends and ultimately, the correct side of the market to be trading with. Using the example of figure 4, taking a long position within the area highlighted in the circle makes no sense since the trend is bearish. You can make a profit taking a long off the bottom of that range but compare the distance the bullish bars travel versus the distance the bearish bars go. Its obvious which direction has the greater odds of success and higher profit potential.

In situations where the trend has turned, you will rarely see the lower and higher timeframes agreeing with each other. Such a situation is confusing to a lot of people. This is what will be addressed next along with market mechanics and its importance.

Chapter 3: Stock Market Mechanics

It might sound like common sense but you'd be surprised just how many traders ignore this. Always know the market you're entering. The stock markets behave very differently from the bond, FX and other esoteric markets. Furthermore, each country's markets have different characteristics that go beyond mere laws and lot sizes. For example, American equity markets have a high proliferation of high frequency traders and algorithmic traders as compared to the European markets.

Each market is a summation of underlying order flow and thus the individual nature of the order flow leaves certain footprints. There are ways of taking advantage of the inherent weaknesses in algorithmic trading but such strategies are well beyond the scope of this book. However, remember that such strategies do no ensure success. Again, the "Holy Grail" approach to trading is the wrong way to go about things. There is no such strategy which will guarantee you win every single trade and make millions within a week. The only way to do so is to cheat. In which case, you don't need this book.

The first thing one needs to understand about the stock markets is that the order book is centralized. The order book, for clarity's sake, is the record of all the orders placed on the exchange. For example: The NYSE and NASDAQ have centralized order books. This has certain advantages and disadvantages for a trader. The advantage is, with the orders being in one place, if one has Level 2 access to the market, a pretty clear picture of the order flow emerges. The disadvantage is, with it all being in one place, everyone can see your orders or even worse figure out your strategy.

Now, a beginner trader with a low 5 figure account need not worry about their strategy being rumbled or their stops being hunted by the bigger players. Frankly, if you think this way, you're giving yourself too much credit. An analogy would be an ocean supertanker diverting its path to either avoid or mess around with a tiny paddle boat. Or to put it in more uncouth terms: Its like an elephant worrying about a fly on its backside. In most cases it just doesn't register or rate any attention. This indicates flaws in your mindset which will be addressed in latter chapters.

The consequence of a centralized order book is that volume data is readily available for any instrument and this can be reliably used as part of your strategy. Another key feature of the equity markets is the extremely strong insider trading laws and disclosure requirements. This will vary based on the country but in developed markets, by and large, there isn't much fraud happening. The penalties simply aren't worth it given that the major players are mutual funds, hedge funds and such financial institutions. No amount of money can repair the damage their credibility would sustain if caught cheating.

This heavy regulation also means brokers and other service providers are largely above board. In the United States, it is absurd these days to think so called "bucket shops" used to exist once upon a time. Again, the penalties are not worth it and the service is oriented towards the customer. The presence of HFT traders though does mean that when trading higher lots, the price will tend to run away from you when entering the market. However, if your account is under USD 5 million, you really needn't worry about this. If your account size is over that, you probably don't need any advice in that regard.

Understanding the margin requirements is crucial for success. You may have a profitable trade going on but if you somehow dip below your margin requirements, your trades will be closed no matter how much profit you might have made. Every market has its own quirks in terms of instruments offered as well. In India for example, there are certain regulations which prevent you from holding a short position overnight. You also need to indicate the time period of the order, that is, if you will be closing out the order intraday or holding it overnight if you're long. This might sound absurd but its pretty progressive compared to Dubai where shorting of any kind is not allowed. My advice is to always start with stocks first and then move onto derivatives. The leverage factor and higher profits in derivatives always attracts the newbies but the risks aren't worth it at the start.

Major news events need to be accounted for such as earnings reports, dividend announcements and splits and mergers.

Generally, it is advised to stay out of the market prior to the announcement and enter only 30 minutes after the event has passed in the case of day trading. If you do have an open position before the announcement, evaluate the existing profit or loss it is in. If it is in a loss, close it out prior to the announcement since there's no sense in risking a bigger loss. If it is in a profit, see how far away from your profit target the price is. If its close, exit the position and bank the profits. If you're slightly better than breakeven, hold onto the position and hope for the best.

In all equity markets, overnight or after hours trading will influence opening prices the following day. This is something unique to these markets and price gaps which will occur at the market open present an opportunity and risk. Personally, I treat the market close as an event and follow the same principles as mentioned in the previous paragraph. If a case for profit exists, it doesn't make sense to close out a position just because a "day trade" is supposed to last a "day".

Another unique feature of stock markets is the correlation between the overall index, sector indices and individual stocks. Now the actual correlation differs in extent for each country's market but suffice to say there's always some correlation. It stands to reason since the overall index is a sum or combination of individual stocks. Hence, before initiating a position, no matter how strong the entry signal is, you must take into account whether you're going with or counter to the major index trend. Admittedly, this is less of a factor in day trading but its something to always keep in mind.

This correlation also helps us unearth opportunities. For example, if the overall market index is looking bullish and if the infrastructure index is bullish as well, there is more reward to be made in going long on the stocks making up the infrastructure index. If the banking index happens to be bearish, the potential rewards of shorting it will be lower since it is counter to the overall market index. Again, the level of correlation varies based on the country. Before entering into it, a trader must know the basic mechanics of this correlation. If there is a high correlation, this needs to be factored into the overall trend determination. That is, treat the overall index direction much like the trend of the higher timeframe.

Speaking of timeframes, the higher timeframes for any equity will overrule the lower timeframe order flow. Due to the compressed nature of the market hours in equity markets (that is, there is a definite open and close), countertrend trading is inadvisable. This doesn't mean you don't engage in it but you have to keep in mind the odds of profit are lower and requires far more work. Generally, I'd advise beginners place 100% of their trades with trend. So in a situation where the trend has turned on the 5 minute chart but hasn't on the 15 minute, wait till it does turn on the 15 minute before going long on the 5 minute. If the higher timeframe is neutral, that is, in a range, and the lower timeframe is bullish, go long by all means since the position isn't against the higher timeframe.

The activity levels of the markets also vary and depend on the types of players involved. In the US and Europe for example there is heavy institutional presence and the markets are quite active except for a few hours around lunch time. In contrast markets in China and India which have a majority retail presence are mostly active at the open and close and that is where the most money is made. When evaluating your trading strategy, its important to keep in mind the time when trades are placed since some strategies work better at the open versus close or middle of the day etc. The general rule of thumb is always trade when volumes are the highest.

By now you might be bored by my spending 3 chapters on the basics and you might be impatient to get to the good stuff, that is, the indicators and strategies which will make you money. Well, that begins from the next chapter on but remember: The basics are called so for a reason. None of the following indicators or strategies will be of any use to you unless you comprehend trend identification, turning points and market mechanics. Most people jump straight to the indicators and blindly implement them since they don't know any better. Don't be that person. Master the basics first and eventually, you won't need anyone telling you which indicator or strategy to use.

Chapter 4: The MACD- Improved

I can hear the groans from all of you. You were promised a new and successful way of trading and here I am introducing the most tired, cliched and common indicator of them all: The MACD. There will be some readers who are unaware of this however, and the next paragraph is for their benefit. Those aware of what this is can safely skip the next one.

The MACD stands for Moving Average Convergence Divergence. It is most commonly pronounced "Mack D" although there are some who pronounce the individual letters out. Briefly, the MACD is a plot which uses 2 moving averages as the input (say the 5 EMA and 20 EMA- designated faster average and slower average) and indicates whether the faster average is above or below the slower average. If its above, the MACD line will have a positive value and negative if below. The idea is, when price starts to rise or fall, the faster, more sensitive average will react first and if it crosses the slower average, it means price is higher/lower than its recent past. The moment the MACD crosses the 0 level is when the faster average crosses the slower one. General opinion is you go long when it crosses 0 to positive value and short when it crosses 0 to negative value.

The conventional way of using the MACD causes a bunch of false signals since it completely focuses on the value of the averages itself without taking into account prevailing market conditions. Not to mention the fact that since everyone and their grandma knows what the MACD is and they're all using it the exact same way, the effectiveness of using this as a strategy fades. This improved strategy however takes into account the basics illustrated in the previous chapters, namely, trend strength and turning points.

The biggest pitfall everyone falls into is using the MACD is turning it into a quest to determine the ideal numbers for the fast and slow moving averages. When this fails to yield results, people turn to the histogram and try to unlock it as if it contains ancient secrets. There is no secret! Its all right there in front of you on the chart! Not realizing this and applying the old way is a surefire way to insanity. Start embracing the new way right now.

Briefly, here are the rules:

1) Determine trend direction.

2) Determine trend strength. You may use a number or have some grade for it or not. The idea is you understand the degree of strength in the direction.

3) Use any faster and slower EMA number in the indicator input. The actual numbers don't matter so long as there's a decent gap between them. Example: 5 and 20.

4) The MACD will cross 0 before price reaches your turning point. The bar after it closes above/below your turning point, enter in that direction at the close of the bar/candle.

5) If price is already past a turning point and in a well established trend, check to see if the MACD is below/above 0 and that it is confirming the direction of entry. That is, if price is below a turning point and a bear trend is on, enter only when the MACD is below 0 and price remains below the turning point.

6) Place your stop based on trend strength. If trend strength is low, that is, there are substantial counter trend players, place your stop above/below a deep support/resistance level. If trend strength is high, place it above/below a closer level.

7) Place your reward at the same distance as your entry is from your stop level after taking into account commissions if trend strength is low. If strength is high, place it at 2X distance. (For example: If stop is at 2 points from entry and trend strength is low, place the take profit order at 2 points from entry. If trend strength is high, place it at 4 points from entry)

8) Do not use MACD if price is in a range. Just do not.

Alternatively, in case trend strength is low, you can opt to wait for a pullback into a deep support/resistance level and enter close to the level. This enables you to have a closer stop and a potentially larger reward target of 3X. The drawback of course is that you might not enter the trade at all since there's no guarantee that price will pull back. It depends on how aggressive you want to be. My advice is to experiment with both ways on a trial account and see which one suits you best. Only then implement this live.

Please understand this is not a 100% guaranteed winning strategy. This is merely an entry signal. Your actual profits depend on your entry, stop loss and your reward points. It also depends on your ability to pull the trigger and see the trade through to the end. Lastly, it also depends on how much work you're willing to put in to work on the basics. The charts in the next few pages illustrate the method.

Figure 5: As price crosses the turning point on the FTSE (indicated by the arrow), we see the MACD value is already negative. Trend strength being pretty strong (notice the lack of bullish bars as it approaches the turning point and how the number of bullish bars are decreasing), we can safely place our stop slightly above the broken turning point level. A maximum reward of 2.5 was available speaking conservatively before price turned back into the level.

Note how at the 2nd arrow, a false long signal is generated. Such signals will occur and are unavoidable. They are the cost of doing business.

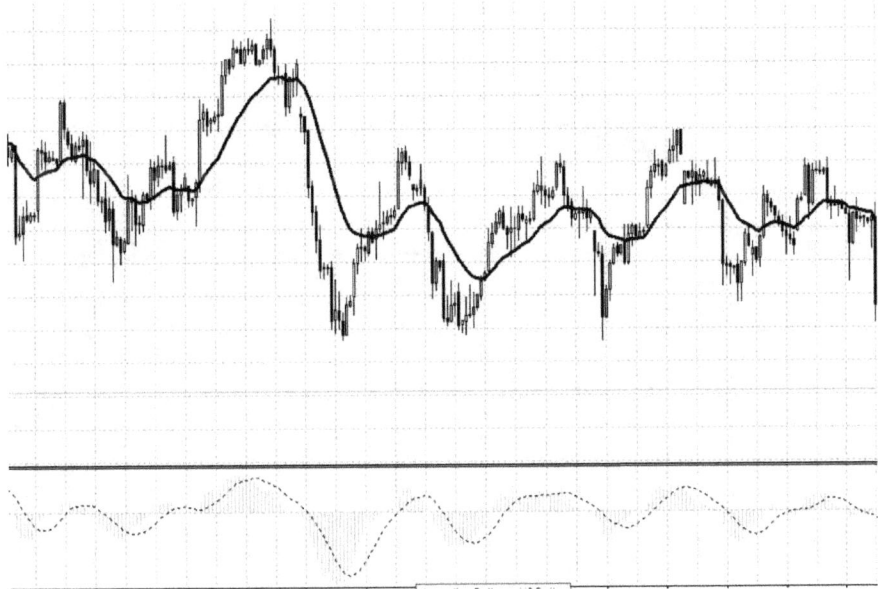

Figure 6: Do not use the MACD in a range. Note the number of times the MACD crosses and re-crosses zero. The number of false signals in incalculable.
Also, since there is no definite trend, there isn't any question of using the MACD to even begin with.

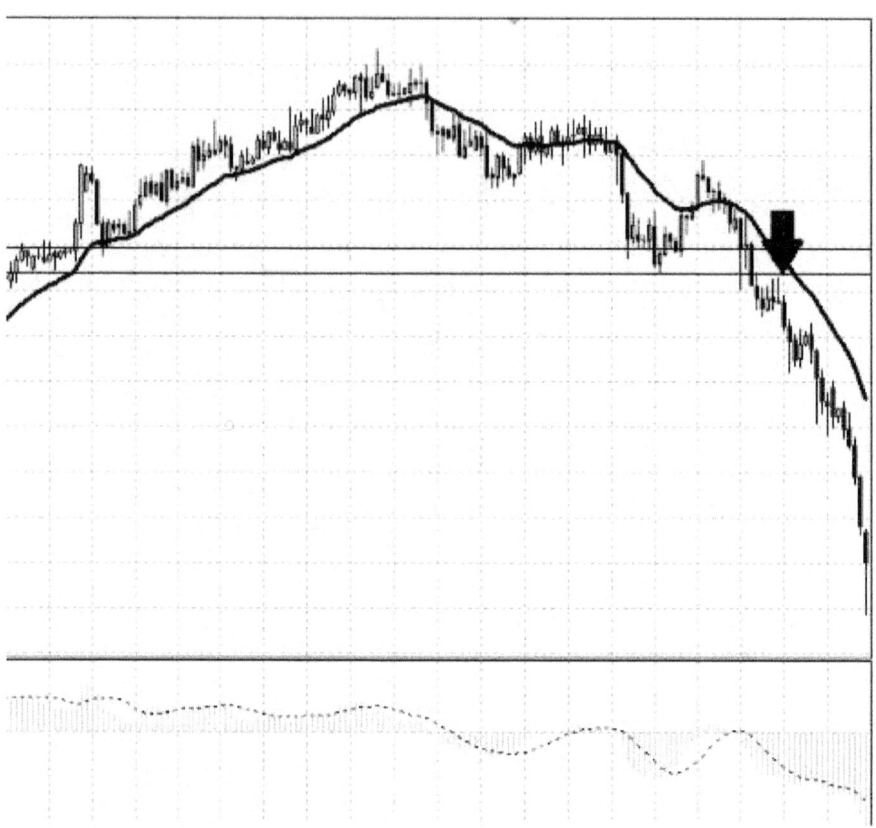

Figure 7: Trend strength will change sometimes and this may cause you to miss entries. Here, after initially showing strong buyer interest prior to the break below the turning point, one might have been tempted to wait for a deeper pullback entry. However, the pullback never materialized.
Decide how aggressive you want to be and trial it first. Implement whichever approach suits you best.

Chapter 5: 20 EMA S/R

As mentioned previously, the 20 EMA is one of the indicators we use to sometimes help determine trend direction. The only reason this is an important indicator is because of the sheer number of traders, both amateur and professional, who implement this as a part of their strategies. The number 20 by itself is not a holy grail and has no real significance.

Often, the 20 EMA ends up behaving as dynamic support or resistance (S/R). This is often the case in trends which have a high degree of trend strength. When trends are heavily imbalanced it doesn't take much to get with trend players on board and the closest S/R often acts as a trend continuation zone. The problem with using the closest static S/R is that different people have different views with regards to the strength of levels on a chart.

Therefore the solution is to use something which everyone agrees on. This is where the 20 EMA is useful. Like a self fulfilling prophecy, its usefulness stems from the fact that everyone thinks its useful. Might sound a bit dodgy but then again, if you think about it, all forms of price work on the same principle.

Executing this strategy requires you to have a very strong ability to identify trend strength. Again, this only comes about as a result of practice. This strategy is a prime example of how mastering the basics, instead of jumping between systems recklessly, is what gives you the big rewards. Also note the simplicity of the system. There's no need to fill your chart space with a ton of indicators or keep staring at the screen endlessly.

Simply assess trend strength and enter close to the 20 EMA as price approaches it. Place your stop below the 20 EMA. The exact location is more of an art than science and is something one must practice on a trial account. Again, you can be aggressive and get real close or be conservative and place your stop a fair distance away. A good rule of thumb is to look at the extent to which the 20 EMA was punctured previously and place your stop at the same distance below the EMA.

Needless to say this strategy does not work in a range or in a trend with low or even medium trend strength. The best way to implement this is to practice on a trial account and develop a feel for it and only then implement it with a live account. Aim for at least a 2X reward with this strategy.

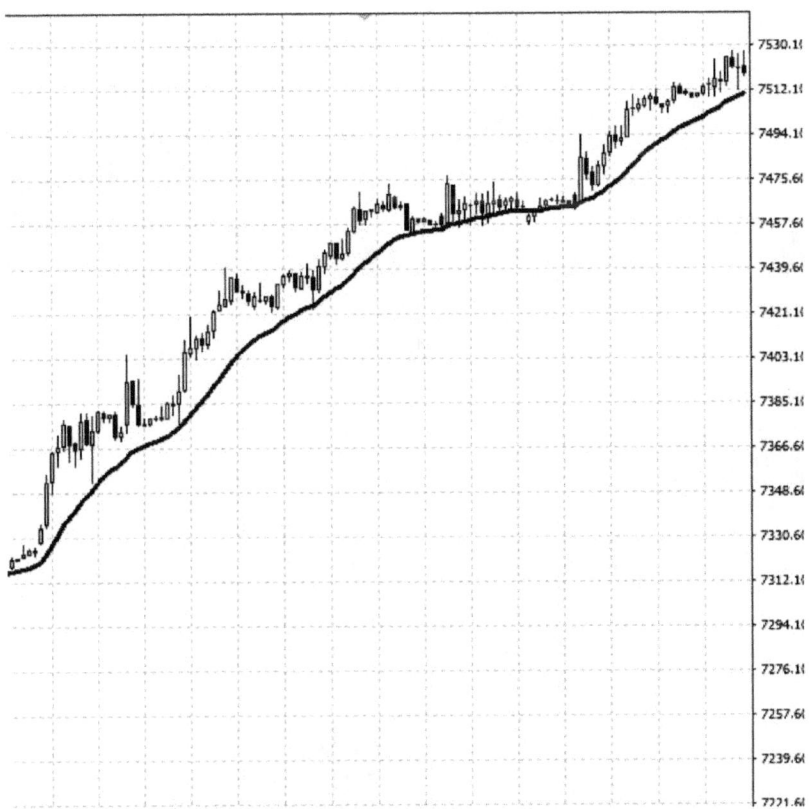

Figure 8: Trend strength is very high with hardly any countertrend players involved. Note how the FTSE constantly bounces off the 20 EMA.
As trend strength decreases, it hangs around longer near the 20 EMA but still doesn't go below it considerably.

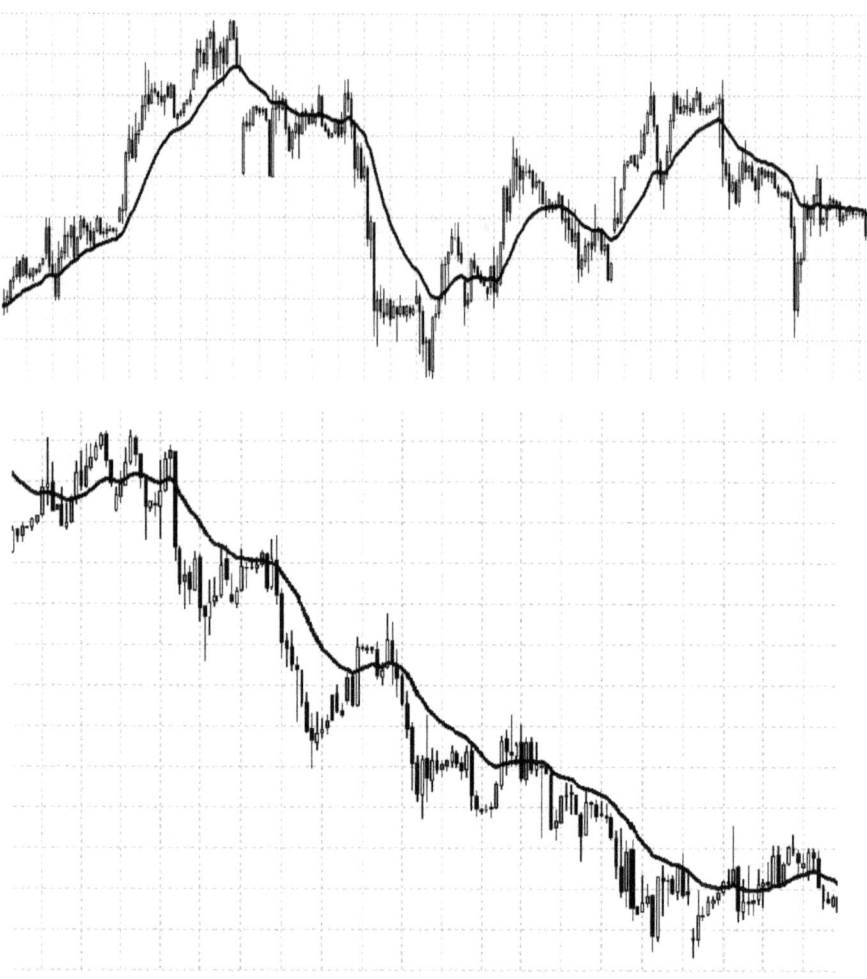

Figure 9: This does not happen in the case of a range (above) or in a trend with medium trend strength (below). The point is to understand the basics and then implement strategies.
Blind application only results in losses!

Chapter 6:
Momentum Patterns

Almost everyone who has dabbled in trading knows and has some experience with patterns. Patterns come in all shapes and sizes and some indeed can be absurd to consider. The truth is all patterns are highly subjective and depend on the trader themselves. Trading is part art and part science. Pattern recognition comes firmly under the artsy part of trading.

If you feel you're more of a visual person then pattern recognition trading might be the way to go. There are a lot of crazy patterns out there but you need to focus on only a few tried and tested ones. These are listed below and we'll take a look at them individually.

1) Cup and Handle

2) Head and Shoulder

3) Ascending triangle

4) Descending triangle

5) Parabolic curve

Day trading is specifically about volatility. The greater the volatility in the markets the greater the chances are of making money. The key to making good money in the markets while day trading is to identify stocks which are making great headway. After all, no one wants to be long of some stock that isn't headed anywhere while the rest of the market is going up 10% or more. The above patterns not only help identify momentum in stock but also generate reliable entry signals. The general rule of thumb with trading patterns is to aim for a reward of 2X risk.

Cup and Handle

The trend strength is a vital aspect of all the patterns we will be discussing in this chapter. The Cup and Handle pattern is called so due to its visual similarity with an actual cup with a handle. This pattern is a great indicator of a potential breakout and a trend reversal. Applying it though requires nuance and a lot of traders apply this blindly without any thought.

This is true of all patterns since most traders forget that successful trading isn't about the ability to draw the prettiest picture on your chart. Its about understanding what's going on behind the scenes that results in the charts we see. This behind the scenes action is clearly decoded using the trend strength approach. Let us consider the shape of the cup and handle. The curved part of this pattern, that is, the cup, occurs because price is going largely sideways and trend strength is low. The handle part of the pattern indicates lower with trend players and increased counter trend strength. In low trend strength environments, as mentioned previously, we always need to be on the lookout for a reversal. It is very important you understand what is being implied here. The pattern is a good indicator because of the underlying price and trend mechanics NOT because it is a magical shape that by itself pushes price upwards.

The Cup and Handle is best used in environments with low trend strength. The pattern is most powerful when the top of the cup is an important level across timeframes and functions as a turning point. The least optimal use of this pattern is as a trend continuation signal, that is, in a range that occurs in an established trend. The reason for this is because the pattern is a great reversal signal and reversals tend to occur as the strength of the counter trend players steadily increases. In a strong trend strength environment, it doesn't make sense to look for reversals.

This is why most traders fail at implementing patterns of any kind. Blindly implementing them without taking into consideration trend mechanics is as useful as drawing random shapes on a chart. The Cup and Handle when implemented correctly is a very powerful signal and trades entered using this pattern tend to have a large reward compared to risk. You can enter based on how aggressive you want to be. Entering prior to the breakout with a stop near the middle of the range is a pretty aggressive approach but has the highest reward to risk ratio. There is a greater chance of failure however. Entering after the breakout on a pullback has greater chances of success but you might end up missing the trend altogether if the breakout is powerful.

My personal opinion is to enter on a stop order just past the range high. This way, you might not get the best price fills but atleast you'll be a part of the trend. Aim for atleast a 2X reward on this pattern.

The Cup and Handle is a bullish indicator. Te bearish version of this indicator is the reverse cup and handle where the cup is inverted. The shape of the pattern doesn't matter as long as you can understand why the shape gets created in the first place and why it indicates what it does.

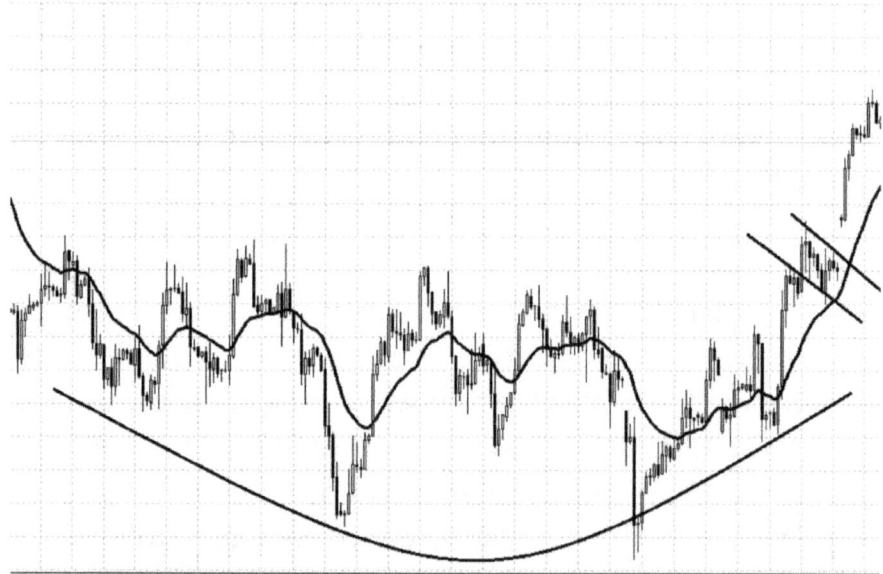

Figure 10: This particular example is an imperfect cup and handle but illustrates how trend strength trumps pretty shapes. Increasing bullish interest helps build the cup shape. The handle is caused by extremly low bearish interest. The level is a turning point given the number of times the bulls were previously rejected around there.
Post the handle, price gaps up the next day and is in a strong bull trend. Your shapes need not be perfect. You understanding of trend strength however does need to be so.

Head and Shoulders

The head and shoulders is perhaps the most quoted and oldest pattern in the history of technical analysis. This is yet another reversal pattern which indicates the end of a bull trend and an impending reversal. The key to using this pattern is to look at the trading volumes on the head versus the shoulders, especially the right shoulder.

The volume should be lower on the bullish bars and greater on the bearish bars on the right shoulder. Again, as with the cup and handle, we see how market mechanics trumps any shape. Lower volumes indicate lower bullish interest and thus causes a reversal. A great optimizer of this pattern is when the base of the structure is a turning point. You can enter on the break of the base or on a pullback into the base. However, this depends on your level of aggressiveness. Aim for atleast a 2X reward with this pattern.

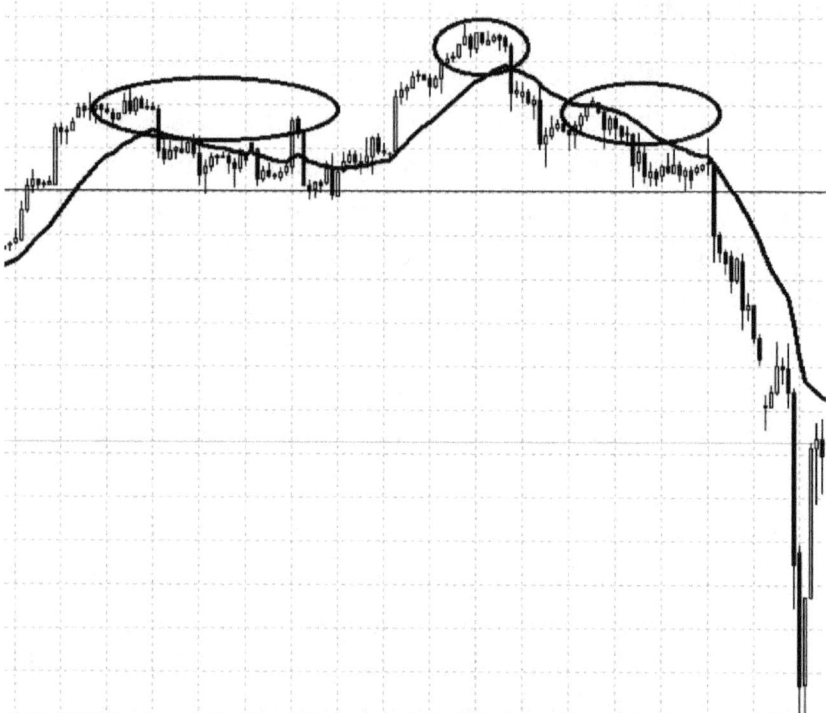

Figure 11: Yet another imperfect shape but if you understand the importance of trend strength, you'll see how significant this pattern is. The 2nd shoulder barely looks like a shoulder but more significantly, the lack of bullish effort speaks volumes. Th subsequent breakout confirms this.

This is a bearish pattern as previously mentioned. The inverse of this is a bullish pattern. Again, don't get caught up too much in the exact shapes and instead understand what causes them in the first place.

Ascending Triangle

This pattern is classified as a continuation pattern as opposed to a reversal pattern like the prior 2 we've looked at. The key point about continuation patterns you need to understand is that you ought to implement them only in medium to strong trend strength environments. Looking for a successful ascending triangle in a low strength environment shows a lack of understanding of how this pattern comes to be in the first place.

In a high strength environment, as price approaches a key resistance level (this pattern applies only to bull trends), the bears push back initially. However, because bullish strength is so high, their efforts eventually peter out and this presents itself as a rising triangle on the chart. A good optimizer of this indicator is to see whether volumes are decreasing on the bearish bars and increasing on the bullish ones. If the volume data is unclear, it isn't a problem since its just an optimizer. The key is to understand the mechanics behind the chart.

Figure 12: The triangle looks imperfect but given the price environment and by gauging the trend strength we realize that the pattern doesn't need to be perfect.
Increasingly lower bearish interest and stronger bullish interest causes price to breakout violently

Again, this pattern works best in a high trend strength environment. There may be isolated cases where it works in a low strength environment but really, you want to put yourself in places where the odds of success are greater. Understanding the order flow that creates this pattern will make it abundantly clear why a high strength environment gives the best odds for this pattern. My preferred entry is a stop order past the top of the triangle with the stop below the prior low within the triangle. Aim for atleast 2X reward with this pattern.

Descending Triangle

Like its bullish equivalent, the descending triangle is a trend continuation pattern and should not be used to predict reversals. The order flow is reversed in this pattern with the bears repelling the bullish efforts and eventually the bear trend continues as pressure builds. The entry and exit methods are the same as for the ascending triangle.

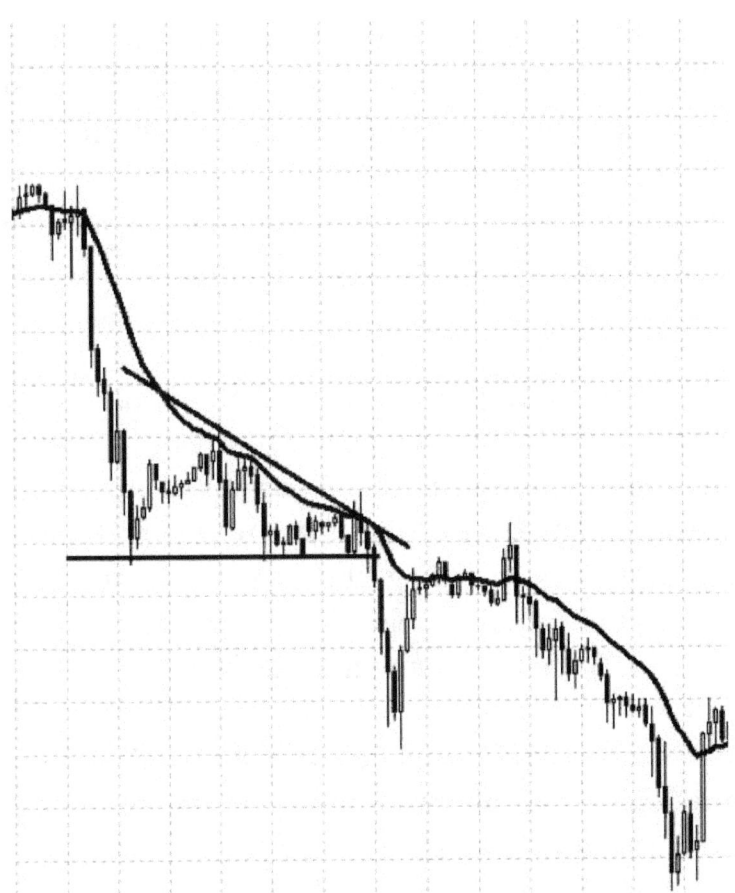

Figure 13: Trend strength is high in this case and subsequent bullish efforts are overcome by the bears until non existent.
Note how the trend strength changes to a medium strength one right after the breakout. This signals to us that the environment is changing and we should be on the lookout for possible reversal patterns.
Needless to say, it is trend strength which forms the basis of everything

Parabolic Curve

Off all the patterns we're looking at in this book, this is perhaps the riskiest of them all but the potential rewards are significant. Ironically this is actually the easiest pattern to recognize and enter from a technical standpoint. The difficulty arises on a psychological level and it is for this reason that the traders who are the most successful at implementing this pattern are either rank beginners or extremely experienced traders. As such I would not recommend trading this pattern unless you have good awareness of your mindset and it weaknesses and have experience in executing a number of traders until you do not have any fear of pulling the trigger.

This is a reversal pattern and often occurs at the end of a euphoric rise or fall. The euphoria attached to the price movement is what gives rise to the opportunity since the trend becomes unsustainable. A key optimizer of this pattern is the presence of a buying or selling climax (covered in the next chapter). More than anything else this signifies that the trend is overextended. Do not make the mistake however of thinking the climax by itself means the trend is at an end. There has to be a steady increase in the angle of the trend until it becomes almost 90 degrees. Ideally you will want to see atleast 3 changes in the angle of the trend.

The trade entry point for this pattern is more of an art than science. You may choose to enter at the close of the bar which breaks the final trendline or you may choose to wait for a mini pullback into the trendline. As with everything else, the reward risk profile changes with entry. The reward, in my opinion, should be atleast 4X risk to compensate for the low hit rate of this strategy. Generally speaking if you can achieve an accuracy rate of 25-30%, you're doing really well.

This brings me back to the point about how psychologically taxing this strategy is. Not only are we trading against a strong trend, we're actually taking on hysteria. It isn't easy to zag when others zig especially when it seems the entire market is against you. As a trader, you need to always be aware of your weaknesses and how the manifest and attack you in any given situation. This is never more true than when trading this strategy. A losing streak of 10-15 trades is quite common and you need to educate yourself on the importance of variance and probabilities in any trading strategy.

Most of all, you need to assess whether this strategy is for you or not. Everyone has different risk profiles and it isn't a negative if you're able to execute certain strategies over others. If anything, doing exactly that is what will ensure success in the markets. Always trial a strategy out extensively and start small. Refer to the chapter on risk management and mindset for more on this.

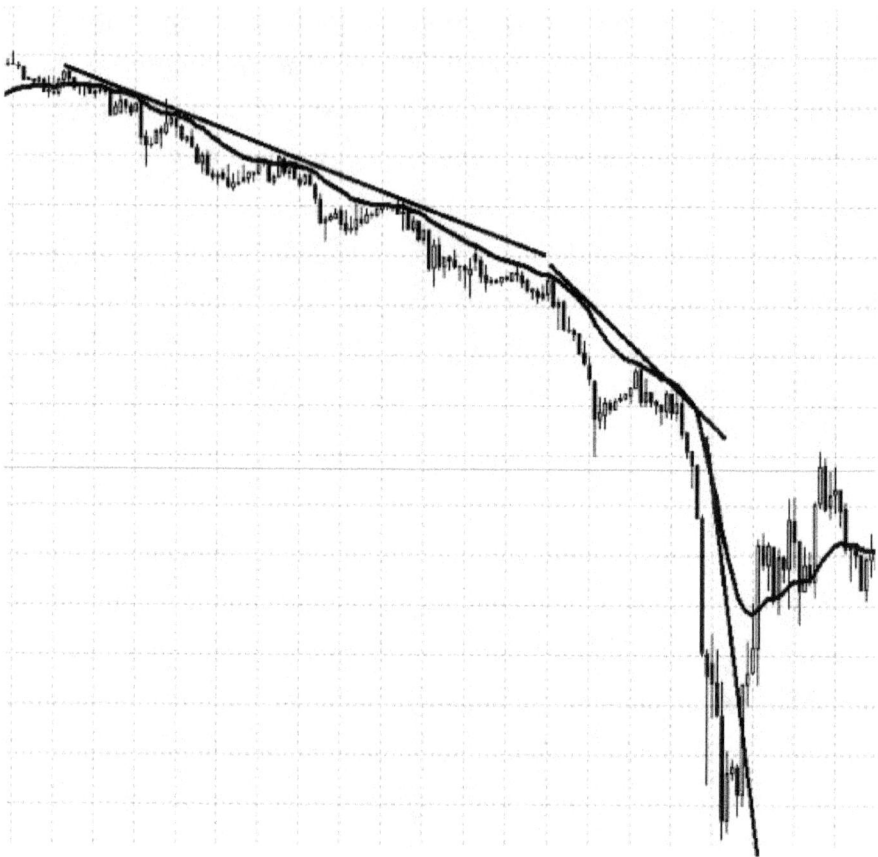

Figure 14: A bearish parabolic arc illustrates both how lucrative and risky this pattern can be. Increasing downside pressure results in a runaway bear trend on the FTSE.
Eventually the trend is unsustainable and a long entry at the break of the last line would have yielded atleast 3X reward speaking conservatively.

Chapter 7: Volume Analysis

Volume analysis is often referred to by different names such as volume spread analysis, volume price analysis or simply, reading the tape. Given the frequency of transactions these days, a physical read of the ticker is pretty much impossible and pointless but analyzing the price chart in conjunction with volume is a tried and tested method. While this subject deserves its own book, I'll cover the salient points in this chapter which will enable you to understand this technique. Taking trend strength into consideration turbo charges this strategy. A word of caution though: this is a highly subjective method and lots of practice is recommended before you take the plunge with real money.

In equity markets, as mentioned earlier, the order book is centralized. This means the volume data we see on our charts can be relied on and it makes any analysis of volumes meaningful. As such this strategy only works in markets which are centralized. This will not, for example, work in the FX market which is decentralized and where nobody has access to the entire trading volume of any instrument.

There is a phenomenon you must understand before proceeding with this strategy. This is often referred to as a climax. Climaxes can be of a buying or selling variation. A buying climax occurs at the end of a bull trend and a selling climax occurs at the end of a bear trend. From an order flow perspective, as a trend progresses, more and more players tend to get on board the gravy train. The longer the trend progresses, the more people enter since it seems like easy money. People have notoriously short memories and soon it seems like this trend will never end. As the hysteria builds and participation in the trend is at its highest, the smart money starts exiting the market recognizing the tell tale signs.

Thus, we see a shift in ownership of the equity from smart to dumb money and eventually a point occurs where the smart money has exited completely and there's no one continuing to prop prices up. This causes a violent correction in the opposite direction and people who entered at the height of the hysteria end up losing their money. No doubt, most of them will at this point complain as to how the markets are rigged against the little guy. There is a kernel of truth in that statement but like I mentioned previously, assuming that big traders are after the little guy's money in the markets is giving the little guy too much credit. Most of the time the need to do so simply doesn't register.

Climaxes have tell tale signs on a price chart. The first indication of a climax is the size of the bars. As a trend progresses and hysteria builds, the size of the price bars increase considerably until finally they become gigantic. This gigantic bar is accompanied by a huge spike in volume. Almost always the next bar is a huge bar in the opposite direction. This indicates the presence of a climax. A bull trend ends in a buying climax and a bear trend ends with a selling climax. Please note: The climactic bar may be either a bullish or bearish one irrespective of the trend direction. That is, a bull trend may have a climactic bearish bar. The key to watch out for is the combination of trend length, the increasing size of the bars and the parabolic nature of the trend culminating in a huge volume spike.

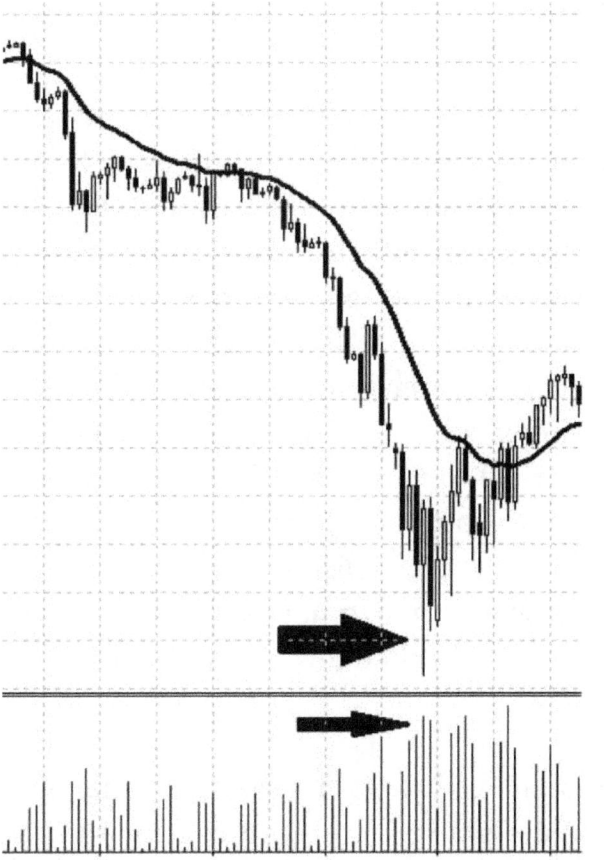

Figure 15: A selling climax on the CAC 40. Notice how volume builds up masively until a collection of bars at the end show huge volume spikes.

Also note how price bounces back up violently post the climax.

In the next few pages, I'll be walking through a chart picked out at random to give you an idea of how to think about volumes in relation to price. I recommend printing out the charts and covering them with a piece of paper so that you do not look ahead and read the text side by side to understand how the thought process works.

We begin with the chart of the CAC40 in Figure 16. An bear trend with strong trend strength is beginning to form. We can infer this by looking at the size of the bars and the relative lack of bullish pushback. Eventually price settles into a range which is marked "Range 1" on the chart. Now as Range 1 progresses, we start to notice a few things. First off, aside from 1 candle initially, there aren't any full bodied bullish candles. In fact most candles seem to have tails or wicks. Given that we're in a bear trend, our primary focus lies in determining whether it is safe to continue trusting the market's direction. Since there isn't any great bullish pushback, we can conclude that the trend strength, though not as strong as previously, is still relatively high and is tilted towards the bears.

Following the candle which gets rejected near the top of Range 1 (marked by a star above it), we can conclude the bears are defending this level pretty successfully and the odds are good that the trend will continue. In addition, with the observations made previously, we can safely decide to enter somewhere near the top of Range 1 with a stop just above it.

Price eventually breaks down and after exiting Range 1, we see a complete absence of bulls. The few bars that do print are minuscule compared to the bearish candles. The volume data also bears this out as the volumes of the bullish candles is far lesser than the volumes of the bearish candles. The trend strength seems to be quite high and we can look forward to a long move downwards. Then out of nowhere at point A, we see a full bodied bullish candle. The volume on this bar isn't very significant though and this points to possible covering of shorts. Either way we need to be on our guard since it seems like the downward momentum is starting to lose steam. Price eventually resumes its downward journey but the volume characteristics are completely different now.

The volumes are collectively a lot larger. Recollect what was mentioned earlier about climaxes and it seems like we're headed towards one soon. Price eventually overextends and snaps back. This is indicated by the bullish bar with the long tail next to the text "Climax 1". We should have been looking to exit much before this and the best way of doing so would be to trail our stop downwards. Given that we would have been in massive profit already, a few extra points in price do not mean much. More money is lost chasing the last few points than anywhere else on the chart.

Following Climax 1, price bounces up aggressively. Now, if the downtrend was parabolic enough, we could have considered a counter trend entry but in my opinion, this particular trend never reached such levels of hysteria. As such, I'd stay out of the counter trend play but more aggressive traders might consider a long somewhere near the climax lows or on the pullback. Either way, we need to recognize that despite the climax occurring we're still in a downtrend with very little strength. Based on principles discussed earlier, we should still be looking to play the short side of the market while on the lookout for the moment when the trend reverses.

Following the principles outlined in the chapter on turning points, we designate point A as the turning point above which we switch our bias to bullish. As described previously, point A is significant because it was the first bullish full bodied bar printed in the downtrend and was perhaps the first place where the shorts started covering their positions. Given how it was swiftly rejected by the bears, it stands to reason this is a significant swing point. Price tries to make it back up to point A but is pushed back down. This is designated as point 1 on the chart. This is a significant point because it shows despite the increasing levels of bullish participation, the bears have enough gas in the tank to push price back down well short of our turning point. An aggressive trader can consider shorting this level with a stop above point A if price reaches this point again.

Volume subsequently shows some interesting characteristics as we see the bearish volumes drop off compared to the previous bullish volumes. This is odd behavior for a bear trend and it confirms our earlier observation about being on the lookout for a reversal. This does not mean however that we start being bullish. Remember the market is a chaotic place and anything can happen. As it is, we leave out bias unchanged. Price eventually makes it back up to point 1 and is swiftly rejected from this level (marked point 2). It eventually makes it back down to the same spot it bounced up from after it hit point 1. We now have 2 hits on top and 2 hits on the bottom and this can be safely called a range.

This doesn't mean we play both sides since we're still bearish. However, the odds are good that the zone around points 1 and 2 is where the sellers are parked and we can safely short from that level. Price bounces up from the bottom of the range and remarkably, with hardly any bearish pushback makes it to the resistance zone. Since we're bearish we can safely enter a short position, however, given the lack of bearish effort in the run up, we place our stop beyond the turning point A. This ensures that our trade will be a loser only if the trend flips. Price gets rejected by the bears yet again at point 3 and this time the bears seem to have woken up as there is hardly any bullish pushback on the way down.

As we reach the bottom of the range, the bulls push back but compare this push upwards to the previous push. The angle is a lot more shallow, the bars are smaller and the length of the pushback is lesser (of course the length is an observation after the fact but the other characteristics can be deduced in real time). This tells us that the odds are good that the resistance zone will hold once more and we can safely short this level at point 4. The bears this time respond in far greater force as can be seen by the volumes to the downside and also the size of the bearish bars and the lack of any bullish bars being printed.

The force of this pushback also tells us the the bottom of the smaller range (marked Level 1) is likely to fold and going long here would be a long shot. There is a weak bounce and price ducks below Level 1 and clears it comfortably on good volumes. Price bounces back up towards Level 1 via a large bullish bar, the first to be printed in a while. This bar naturally warrants some examining and while the size is significant, the volume tells us a different story. We already know the bears are firmly in control and have forced price below a minor level (Level 1) on this timeframe. If the bulls wish to push price higher they'll have to come out in force to break back above Level 1. This means there ought to be significant volume for this to happen. This doesn't seem to be the case here. Therefore on a lower timeframe, we can consider this a level to short. Circumspect traders can choose to wait for a second hit on this level before shorting.

I mention shorting on a lower timeframe simply because the picture will be clearer there. On this timeframe, Level 1 is a minor level in the middle of a range. If we enter on a lower timeframe, we have the opportunity to fine tune our entry and stop to extract maximum reward. Price does get rejected from Level 1 and as it makes its way back down towards the climax levels, we see the bulls step in again. They push price back up towards Level 1 from which we consider a short once again. Price launches itself into Level 1 via a big bullish bar but gets rejected. Price pushes a bit further into the Level 1 zone before turning downwards with good volumes. However, as it approaches the climax level, the bulls again step in and push it higher.

This time though, we see the bulls push it for far longer and without any bearish pushback which is the first time this has happened. This tells us that Level 1 might be in danger. Aggressive traders can short Level 1 once more if they so choose. A tighter stop and reward makes the most sense. Price bounces back down twice and then comes right back to Level 1. This is the first time price has not made a lower low on a rejection from Level 1. It might still do so but given what we've already observed, the odds are good that Level 1 will fold. Any open shorts need to be covered now.

Price does break above Level 1 and after that proceeds without any resistance from the bears all the way back towards our bigger resistance zone. Given its prior history, a short is in order and we do so at point 5. Price behaves very differently though. At point 4, it was swiftly rejected downwards but this time it stubbornly hangs around in the zone before halfheartedly making its way back down. There isn't much bearish presence as evidenced by the lower volumes to the downside as compared to the move up from the climax level as well as the lack of any full bodied bearish candles save for one. This is communicating to us that the bulls seem to be in charge and its a matter of time before they break the resistance zone.

We do not know when this will happen so I would recommend shorting the resistance zone until this does so. As Figure 16 ends, we see price once again stubbornly clinging to the resistance zone and it also appears the 20 EMA is squeezing it against the level. Our open short position may have to be closed out soon or at the very least re-evaluated.

This concludes our look at reading charts using the volume and price method. It requires a lot of training and practice to be able to see things clearly. However, when combining this with the principles of trend strength and turning points, it gives us a full picture of the market and places us automatically on the right side. Even more crucial, impending turnarounds become even more apparent and any potential losses can be cut. As mentioned in the beginning, an entire book can be written on this topic and as such this chapter was to give you all the salient points of this method. There isn't any greater secret to this method. The only difference between someone who is an expert at this versus the novice is the significance attached to certain bars.

As you proceeded through the previous chart, ask yourself which bars do you think are significant as compared to the ones I highlighted. Ask yourself how they helped you form the bigger picture and whether they helped you make clearer decisions. Most of all, avoid the mistake of attaching significance to a bar based on what has subsequently happened to the right hand side of it. Remember, when trading live, you only have the left hand side for reference!

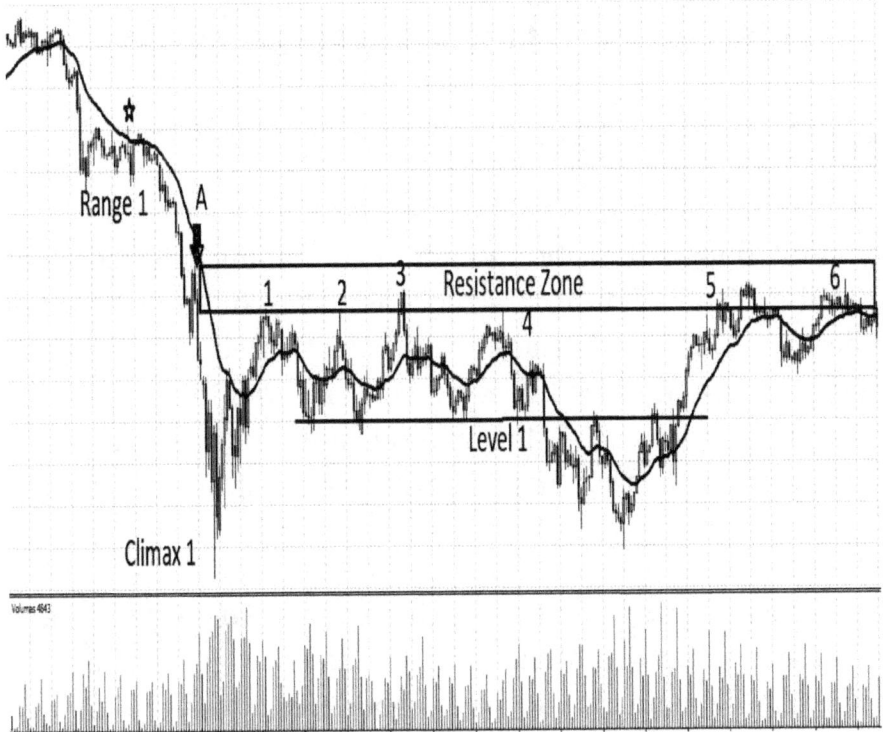

Chapter 8: Accumulation and Distribution

Accumulation/Distribution or more commonly referred to as Acc/Dis is an indicator which is derived from another indicator. On the surface this might seem a result of overthinking and indeed, it is 2 levels removed from the actual price, in reality Acc/Dis has a good rate of success in equity markets or any market that is derived from equities.

The indicator itself works as both as a convergence and divergence indicator. What this means is, it can be used to confirm an existing trend when both the indicator line and price converge. It can also be used to predict a trend change when the indicator line and price diverge from one another. Most traders tend to superficially use this line without any form of other analysis. Most traders also happen to lose money.

Given that it is 2 levels removed from price, this indicator is not a fool proof method and you will not receive any crystal clear signal. Used in conjunction with a prior understanding of trend strength or any form of price action methods, this indicator gives us a deep insight into the behind the scenes action. Simply put, we get to know if the stock we're looking at is being accumulated, or bought in preparation for a rise, or being distributed, that is, being sold in anticipation of a fall.

Accumulation and distribution (the act of buying and selling, not the indicator) tends to play out within ranges. In the previous chapter, the range we looked at was a classic example of accumulation. The sellers exhausted themselves in the trend and the buyers stepped in and steadily overwhelmed the sellers. While we don't know what the conclusion to that story was, given the behavior of the price, its safe to say a breakout probably followed the range.

As a general rule, this indicator is of most use when price is moving sideways after a trend. We can then check to see if the indicator is converging with price or diverging. For example, if price is making new highs but the indicator is actually trending lower, this is a clear divergence and points to the stock being sold on the way up by the smart money. The best approach would be to anticipate price breaking below the trend turning point and short it once it does that. While the trend strength approach directly gives you this information, using the indicator adds an extra layer of confidence. Plus, much like with the 20 EMA, if the price bars are unclear, we can always look to this for greater clarity.

You might be wondering, from the previous example, why not short the stock immediately as the divergence is spotted? The reason is, as mentioned previously, the indicator is 2 levels removed from price. This makes it notorious for giving false signals. This is actually a good thing since most traders use the indicator as a crutch instead of actually bothering to learn market mechanics. Again, the Holy Grail approach, more than anything else, is what dooms most traders from the outset.

There are no real rules for entry and stop placement since the indicator serves more as a warning signal. Actual trade entry and stop placement needs to be based on the trend strength. Using the method outlined in the chapter on the improved MACD should give good results. Indeed, a combination of all the strategies described thus far will give great results. You just need to decide which one fits you the best given your risk appetite and psychological makeup.

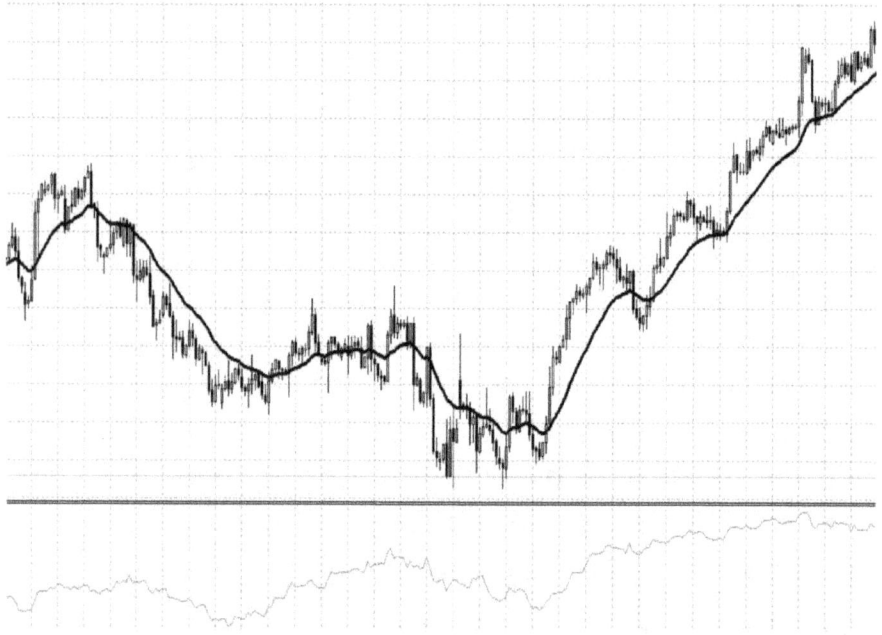

Figure 17: The FTSE shows a clear divergence from the A/D line in the middle of this chart. While the index makes new lows, the A/D actually makes a higher high. This puts us on attention for a price break above the turning point and indeed price does break through.

Chapter 9: Risk Management

You might be tempted to think we've made it back to the boring part of the book now that the indicator and strategy section is finished. The truth is, along with the basics, this is perhaps the one thing that will ensure your success more than anything else. Consider this: Great risk management can mitigate a mediocre strategy but poor risk management will certainly ruin a great strategy.

If you're familiar with trading and have read multiple books on the subject, chances are most of them boil risk management down to your risk per trade, stop loss and position size etc. The reward risk ratio is often presented as the catch all solution to understanding risk management. The truth is the risk reward ratio of your strategy is merely the starting point. Risk in trading contains both quantitative and qualitative aspects. In this chapter, my aim is to enlighten you on both aspects of this. First, let us look at the quantitative aspect.

Quantitative Risk

Any trading strategy, if it needs to be successful, needs to have an edge. This edge can be measured at it most basic level using 2 key statistics, namely, the reward/risk ratio (hereby referred to as R) and your win rate percentage. Most traders get hung up on either one of these numbers and neglect to understand that these 2 work in tandem. One affects the other. A typical newbie is someone who aspires to a 100% win rate and a 5R+ ratio. This is some Alice in Wonderland level of thinking and is practically impossible.

The more realistic way of approaching this is to first of all determine, given your R per trade, what is the minimum win rate you need to breakeven? Notice I said breakeven, not make millions. Your first goal, if you're struggling for consistency and to make money, is to simply breakeven. The progression usually goes as follows: losing lots of money--> losing a little--> breakeven--> making a little money-->making lots of money. You cannot aspire to jump to highest level directly if you're stuck in the lowest level. There is no jumping steps with trading. You need to put in the work and only focus on what you need to do next.

The calculation for this breakeven rate is fairly simple. If you're making 2R per win (that is, you're making on average, twice the amount you lose on average, everytime you have a winning trade), you will need a win percentage of around 35%. The calculation is pretty simple: say on 10 trades you win 3 and lose 7 with 2R per win. So your losses come to (7*1)= 7R. Your winners come to (3*2)= 6R. Your profit and loss is 6R-7R= -1R. So if you're risking 2% per trade, over 10 trades you can expect to lose 2% with this strategy.

Now, its important to note, when starting out, you will not have much of a base to calculate these numbers. You will need a minimum of 100 trades to reasonably calculate these ratios with accuracy. Therefore, my advice when you've placed under 100 trades is to risk as little as possible on your trades. I personally risk 0.5% per trade. There are a lot of trading authorities out there which say risking 2% per trade is perfectly fine but this is hogwash. You will find the vast majority of professional and successful traders risk anywhere from 0.25% to 1% per trade. The successful trader who risks 2% is an outlier.

Your first action upon reading that would probably have been to do some quick mental math and realize you cannot make millions a year with your capital size by doing that. This is indicative of a flawed mindset which needs some fixing. The good news is it doesn't take much to fix this. I'll address this in the next chapter on mindset and how to correctly think about success in trading. The truth is, the correct approach to trading is to constantly cover your downside all the time. Most people only think of the upside and their winners. The successful trader always covers risk and the downside before turning her attention to the upside.

Those of you familiar with the writings of Benjamin Graham may recognize this thought process. This is nothing but the "Margin of Safety" in action. This is a principle which is good enough for some of the greatest investors of all time. It ought to be good enough for you as well. There's no need to waste time reinventing the wheel. Just follow the process and you will get there. Those of you worrying about how you will get rich with this sort of trading, please be patient. I address this point in the final chapter.

Getting back to our quantitative look at risk, once you've placed atleast 100 trades risking under 0.25% per trade, you will be able to have relevant stats on your strategy and trade process. As I said previously, the win rate and R is the bare minimum you have to look at. You need to further dig into your numbers and understand the variance of your results. I'm not going to bore you with the statistical definition of variance but will instead illustrate what this practically means.

Let's say you're on a losing streak. Indeed if your trading strategy has a win rate of 35%, you will lose far more than you win and losing streaks of 2-3 trades are extremely likely. This is where struggling traders fail. Once the losing streak starts, they start tinkering with the strategy, assuming something is wrong. This is indicative of a Holy Grail mindset and as I've mentioned previously, this is completely the wrong way to go about trading. The correct approach is to understand what are the odds of such a losing steak occurring?

That is, with a 35% win rate, what are the odds of having a losing streak of 2 trades? 3 trades? 10 trades? I'm not going to disclose the answers to those questions here because once you search for them yourself, you're likely to be shocked. Briefly, it is extremely likely you will have a losing streak of atleast 8 trades with a win rate of 35%. Only when your losing streak becomes of such a size that it is improbable, should you start looking at your trade process. Until then, you need to remain aware of what your odds are at all times.

This is what it means to think in probabilities in trading. Most authorities simply make that statement and leave it hanging without further explanation. Trading is about being aware of your probabilities at all times. You may have noted in the section on the trading strategies, I never once indicated that any strategy is a sure shot or is foolproof. I even gave examples of when a given strategy fails. This is because I'm not concerned with how much of a sure shot a strategy is. I'm only concerned with what the win rate needs to be and how much R do I need to make on that strategy to make money. If I cannot make those numbers work for me after a sizeable sample, I drop it. This is how a professional thinks and it is crucial for you to adopt this method of thinking.

Understanding variance is a key part of evaluating your current strategy. Its not all doom and gloom though. For all the odds of a losing streak there are odds of a win streak as well. The number of wins in the streak will be smaller of course but when you factor in the 2R reward per win, you're making pretty good money on those streaks. I'll bet none of you will mind experiencing variance via a win streak. You shouldn't mind experiencing it via a losing streak either. This is an unnatural way of thinking and is something I'll address in the chapter on mindset.

Another key variable to look for is the consistency of your risk management. Now this can't be boiled down to a number but basically, you need to look at your losses and check if they are consistently around your risk percent per trade. So if you've decided to risk 0.25% of your account per trade, how many losing trades are actually at or below this number? If your losers are all over the place but average out to 0.25%, that is frankly, terrible risk management. It means you're likely adding to your losers and engaging in wishful and emotional thinking every time you enter a trade. The successful trader is someone whose losses show a consistent risk percentage of their account. So if they decide to risk 0.25%, their losses will be 0.25% or less. Enforcing discipline in this regard will do wonders for your strategy.

Another bogus piece of advice I've seen floating around recently is the thought that you should risk a fixed amount per trade versus a fixed percentage of your account. Risking a fixed amount violates the very basis of risk management which is covering your downside. It means in a losing streak you're actually risking a bigger percentage of your account and in a win streak you will be risking a smaller percentage as the streak lengthens. This is getting the worst of both worlds: losing more in a losing streak and winning less in a win streak. I really hope I don't need to further explain how stupid this piece of advice is. Some proponents of this method will argue it gets you out of drawdowns (that is, when your account balance dips below its peak equity value) faster. My response is, drawdown recovery is a function of variance, not some BS risk per trade formula.

Since we're on the subject, drawdowns are an important statistic to measure as well. No account in the world is on a continuous upward 45 degree angle. You will have peaks and valleys. A drawdown is essentially the length of that dip, measured as a percentage from the peak equity value and also as time, that is, measuring it in days and months. You will also need to measure recovery time which is the length of the upward swing past the old equity high from the bottom measured in days. A good system will have a faster recovery time as compared to the drawdown time.

The percentage of drawdown matters as well. As a daytrader, you should be aiming for less than 5% drawdown per month. If you're starting out, I recommend a drawdown limit of 3%. Yes, that is a limit. It means you will stop trading when you breach it. You need to have a drawdown limit for a day, week and month. Your daily limit can be defined as either a percentage or as the number of consecutive losses. For example if you lose 6 in a row, you cease trading for the day. I'm not saying 6 is a magic number, you will need to work out how much that means as a loss percentage given your risk per trade. Enforcing this requires discipline and awareness. Violate this and you will not succeed. Its really as simple as that. If you're still not convinced consider this: Even Usain Bolt had bad days at the track. What makes you think you will have only good days in the market? Recognize when things are bad and exercise the option Bolt never had. You have the choice to take part or sit out.

Another informative statistic is the length of winners and losers measured as the time the trade was active. If your losers are far shorter in time than your winners, for example, perhaps you're placing your stops too close and not giving your trades room to breathe. Also look at how long your losers were in positive territory. If the majority of your losers, for example, tend to reach around 1.5R and then turn back, either your stops are too wide or perhaps you'd be better off targeting 1.5R instead of a higher ratio. You will be compensated because you'll have a higher win rate.

Qualitative Risk

Looking at risk qualitatively is a bit more difficult for beginners since most of them have never thought of risk in such terms or ever thought of risk as a function of discipline. Indeed most unsuccessful traders, whether beginners or experienced, tend to think of trading as having a successful strategy. They do not pay heed to risk management or mindset. They define an "edge" as how often the strategy wins or how much better it is or how it is some secret sauce that no one has discovered. The reality is, in this age of constant information, it is impossible for some secret sauce to exist indefinitely. Successful trading is indeed having an edge. Your edge, though, is made up of a number of things. It means executing your strategy perfectly. It means risking the correct amounts per trade. It means thinking the correct way about success (addressed in the next chapter).

Successfully executing this edge is a matter of preparation. Ask yourself, how well do you prepare for your trading day?

Do you roll out of bed an hour before the open and sit down munching your breakfast and coffee while looking at your charts? Do you even consider things such as: How well did you sleep? How physically fit are you? What is your current mental state? Are you going through a tough period in your life that needs addressing? Have you practiced your technical skills? Are you aware of how your weaknesses will attack you today? And so on.

Make no mistake, to trade successfully you need to approach your trading day with as much precision as an athlete approaches game day. Using the previous example of Usain Bolt, do you really think he ever showed up to a race hungover? Do you really think he didn't practice extensively before hand and execute his workout strategy? Do you think he ignored his nutrition needs? (notwithstanding his claim of eating Mcdonalds). Do you think he was out until 3 A.M the day before a race? Most of all, do you think he changed his methods of preparation simply because he was having a bad day? Do you think he did things differently before every race or did he do the exact same things over and over again?

These questions answer themselves. If you think you do not need to prepare for your trading day, you might as well flush your money down the toilet, you'll at least learn a lesson that way. Preparing well gives us confidence in our abilities and lessens the impact of losses since we know deep down there isn't anything we could have done better. It gives us a marker as to where our abilities are and what we need to do next. So what constitutes as good preparation?

To sum it up in a sentence: You need to ensure your mind is as close to its peak cognitive ability as possible. There will always be distractions and tough periods in our lives but you have to make sure you have a way to put them aside when trading. You need to evaluate if you have the ability to do this. The death of a loved one, for example, is impossible to put aside for most people. An argument with your spouse/girl/boyfriend though is somewhat more manageable for most. The point is you need to be aware of yourself and make a call. I highly recommend engaging in physical exercise and some form of meditation or mindfulness prior to the trading session. This ensures our bodies and minds get a workout and it refreshes us. I don't believe I need to go into detail about the benefits of exercise and meditation.

Ensure you get quality sleep every night. Do what you need to do to ensure this. If you miss exercising for a day, you can get by. Miss a night's sleep though and you're effectively a zombie. Take some time during the day to also practice your strategy. There will be core elements to it and keep reinforcing and practicing these basics. Should you choose to follow the trend strength approach, you will need to constantly practice this skill in the beginning. The best way to practice is on a simulation software or on a demo account, although the latter is a bit slower in terms of reps received.

As you can see, not executing these steps correctly will leave you below your peak ability and trading without taking care of these things is akin to jumping into a sea of sharks with bloody meat strapped to you. Execute these to the best of your abilities and don't worry about anything else. If your mind is too unfocused simply walk away and come back the next day. The market won't go anywhere. If you choose to ignore this aspect, you're running huge risks and no amount of quantitative statistics will save you.

Executing all of this starts with your mindset which is what we'll look at next.

Chapter 10: Mindset and Success

There is a belief prevalent in society that success in any field is a result of a person having some form of innate talent that they were born with. This belief causes us to think that if we don't have some magically presented talent towards something we are doomed to failure. A great writer is great because she was born having a talent for words, a musician was born with a talent for music and so on. This belief has completely warped our definition and expectations of success and has caused more failure than anything else.

Another toxic belief is one regarding hard work. Success, the belief goes, is a direct result of lots and lots of hard work. Put in the hard yards and its impossible to fail. There is some truth to this but in my experience, this statement overlooks a number of things, most specially, the nature of the work. People have been conditioned to believe now, because of these omissions, that mere hard work will guarantee success. In this age where computers are poised to take over a majority of low level jobs, nothing is further from the truth. Hard work is necessary, but it needs a proper channel.

Confidence is something else that is misunderstood. With regards to trading, confidence is something most struggling traders believe they will acquire once they start making money. They claim to not be confident in their strategy unless it makes them money. They build castles in the sky of how once they start making money, they'll execute flawlessly and manage risk well and live happily ever after. In the here and now though, they continue to lose money and keep blaming wrong strategies and the market and everything else under the sun.

These 3 qualities and beliefs, those regarding talent, hard work and confidence, underline our most basic beliefs about the world and ourselves. These beliefs exist on a sub conscious level and make themselves heard in ways which we cannot fathom unless we achieve a greater sense of awareness with regards to what is going on inside our minds. If you have the wrong beliefs, it doesn't matter what your strategy is or how good your risk management is, you will never be successful. Let's look at them one by one.

Talent and the need for it

How many times have you looked at a sportsperson doing something great and though "wow, they're incredibly talented" instead of thinking "wow, their mindset is so strong"? The harsh truth is talent doesn't count for much in the overall scheme of things. Sure, at the highest level of any endeavor, talent and genetics does provide a slight edge over the competition if everybody is executing at the same degree of efficiency. It does not however guarantee a path to success. The most talented person still needs to work hard. For example, most people look at the fact that Mozart became famous for his music at the age of 18 and put it down to some innate genius alone. The truth is, by the age of 18, Mozart had been composing music for over 13 years starting from the age of 5. He worked relentlessly on his craft and by the time he was 18, he was as experienced as any adult composer was. Thinking that Mozart simply rolled out of bed and became famous is absurd.

We recognize this absurdity on a conscious level but most of believe the exact opposite in our sub conscious minds. Guess what? It is our sub conscious minds that make up the majority of our thoughts, over 90% in fact. All of our actions are informed by the sub conscious and as long as you have this belief within you, you will continue to behave in ways that make it true. You will create a reality which conforms to your beliefs about the world.

The truth is, we do not need some God given gift to be successful traders. You do not need a math, science or financial background. Certain trading strategies do require you to be good at math and have an analytical background but the beauty of the markets are their diversity. You are free to adopt any strategy you choose. The success of that strategy depends on how perfectly you execute it, how well you manage risk and what you believe about yourself to be true. Where does talent come into that equation?

The world of sports is full of examples of conscious hard work triumphing over talent. If you're a fan of the NFL, you certainly know the story of Tom Brady. Here's a guy who went from being a scrawny backup on a team that had no wins in high school, to being the greatest QB of all time, supermodel wife and all. What do you think carried him to the highest level of his sport? Was it talent? Or was it his relentless pursuit of his vision and his willingness to execute whatever task was necessary? In the previous chapter, I outlined the basic outline of how to prepare for a trading day and the variety of ways in which you need to manage risk. If Brady were an unsuccessful trader, how do you think he would have reacted to that advice? How did you react to it when you first read it?

Michael Jordan, who needs no introduction, has repeatedly stressed how it was hard work and practice that made him the greatest. Not his talent. Trading is no different. You need to scrub this belief from you that you need to be talented to be a successful trader. We'll discuss some ways to install new beliefs at the end of this chapter but for now, please keep in mind that talent is overrated. It is perfect execution that always wins.

Hard Work and Success

Now there is no doubt that hard work brings success. Most people though develop an expectation of success just because they put in hard work. They end up working longer and more often and when success doesn't come they find themselves burned out and at their wits end. The reality is, hard work is but a part of the success formula. More pertinently, hard work done with the correct intention and towards the correct direction is what brings success.

You can sit there and stare at charts all day and consider it hard work. It certainly is. However, if you haven't decided on what it is you wish to achieve from looking at the charts, your work is of no use. You need to have a plan in place before you sit to work. Before you practice, you have to make a list of what your weaknesses are and work on those exclusively for that session. When you're trading the markets on demo prior to going live, you need to be conscious of what you're doing this for. You cannot tell yourself that you'll be more serious or execute better when you go live. Your execution has to be perfect and you need to do it repeatedly.

Hard work channeled in the right direction will always bring results. Now, there's no guarantee those results will be positive. However with a mindset that values learning over results, you will always move forward because you'll recognize even negative results make you stronger and better. Your work should be focused on improving your ability to execute better. So this means you train yourself to become an expert on your entry and exit signals, you train yourself to become aware of your thoughts and beliefs, you train yourself to implement methods to overcome or mitigate the harmful effects of said beliefs and you train yourself to be disciplined with your risk management. Directed this way, the work you put in will ensure your success.

Confidence

Much like unsuccessful traders think they'll magically execute better in realtime versus demo, many think they'll become confident in themselves and their strategy once the results start coming in. The reality is the other way round. Results come from the confidence in your abilities and your strategy. Using the previous example, do you think Tom Brady's confidence in himself dips when he throws an interception or loses a game? Do you think he starts thinking and adjusting his throwing mechanics when he tosses a pick? How about when he throws a touchdown? Does his confidence in himself rise or fall or does it remain the same as it was?

There's a valuable lesson here. Your results cannot dictate your confidence level in anything. Confidence need to be innate otherwise you'll be a slave to world and no one wants to be in that position, constantly rising and falling based on what others think of you. You need to have the belief that you will overcome challenges no matter the obstacle. Your mindset needs to be solution oriented, that is, you need to focus on the solution to your problems instead of the problems themselves and how they make you feel.

When under pressure, we tend to default to our ingrained mental programming. This means when you're trading, which is a pressure packed environment, you will default to your innate confidence level. If this is high, well and good, but if you're like most people, you'll start looking for results to justify feeling good about yourself and this leads to over trading, chasing wins and generally screwing up your strategy.

Focus on executing your strategy perfectly instead and focus on your belief in being able to overcome challenges, and you will achieve success. Below are some techniques to instill confidence in yourself and to root out toxic beliefs:

1) Visualize yourself being confident in the markets and executing flawlessly. Focus on things you can control.

2) Visualize accepting losses as cost of doing business and how your confidence level remains the same regardless of results.

3) If you aren't a visual person write out statements that confirm the above beliefs.

4) Prepare a trading plan which includes your plan to practice your skills and follow it.

5) Practice some form of meditation.

6) Start observing how you react under pressure. Observe and note down the symptoms. When they occur once more consciously turn your focus onto executing your strategy.

7) Inform someone close to you about your intent to eradicate incorrect beliefs. Have them prompt you anytime you say or do something which goes against what you want to achieve.

8) Practice gratitude.

The topic of mindset is a vast one and entire volumes of books have been written about this. The material outlined above is a starting point and can be seen as the bedrock from which to build. You will always face challenges but remember, our response to the challenge is always a choice. Focus on what you can control and hope for the best with regards to what you cannot.

Chapter 11: How to Make Millions

Hopefully you've come to recognize how successful trading is a process and not some unattainable myth. Remember, you're always a lot closer than you believe. The key to successful trading is executing a number of steps flawlessly. If "flawlessly" seems a bit daunting, then remember that you can train yourself to do so. You don't need some special talent or secret ingredient to become successful.

Trading will offer you huge monetary rewards but most people have the wrong ideas as to the nature of those rewards. Let's get this out of the way first. You will not make a million within a year starting with a low 5 figure account. Consider this: the greatest investor of all time, Warren Buffett, has averaged a 20% annual return in his career. Let that sink in for a second. When anyone tells you they can sell you a system that guarantees 20% a month, run for the hills.

Don't be discouraged though. While you cannot live on 20% of a 10k account, if you establish a good track record which demonstrates excellent risk management and consistent execution, you will not have to go searching for capital. It will flow to you. Financial institutions are always on the lookout for good traders. By establishing a good track record (about a year) with your own money, you will demonstrate your ability to trade well and can apply for trading jobs at institutions and proprietary trading firms. The path to a professional trading career isn't that improbable coming from a retail trading background. Managing an 8 figure account within 3 years of a successful track record isn't far fetched. Do you think you can live on 20% of the gains of an 8 figure account?

All you need to do is follow the principles of successful trading as outlined previously. Focus on your execution and be aware of your mindset.

Last of all, have faith that the universe is looking out for you. You'll be fine no matter what happens. So remind yourself of that fact and get to work. I wish you the best of luck!

If you think this book has helped you gain any insight at all, please do leave a review on Amazon. If you feel this book was rubbish, leave one anyway. I will sincerely appreciate your feedback.